To _____

From _____

Other giftbooks by Helen Exley:
Happy Birthday to a super Brother
Mothers …
Sisters …
When Love is Forever

Published simultaneously in 1996 by Exley Publications in Great Britain, and
Exley Giftbooks in the USA.
Copyright © Helen Exley 1996

12 11 10 9 8 7 6 5 4 3 2 1

Border illustrations by Juliette Clarke
Edited and pictures selected by Helen Exley

ISBN 1-85015-797-9

Designed by Pinpoint Design.
Text research by Margaret Montgomery.
Picture research by J. M. Clift, Image Select, London.
Typeset by Delta, Watford.
Printed in Singapore

Exley Publications Ltd, 16 Chalk Hill, Watford, Herts. WD1 4BN.
Exley Giftbooks, 232 Madison Avenue, Suite 1206, NY 10016, USA.

Brothers!

QUOTATIONS SELECTED BY
*H*ELEN *E*XLEY

EXLEY
NEW YORK • WATFORD, UK

No-one can understand as you do – for you shared my beginnings, know the same joys, faced the same terrors. We do not have to explain to one another, words are not necessary. Our lives are interlocked.

PAM BROWN, b.1928

A BROTHER DOESN'T LIKE little children
or a fussy mother. A brother
is one of the worst people in the world.
Sometimes a brother is
kind and helps you annoy your sister.

ALEX WHEATCROFT, AGE 10 YEARS

I'm glad I've got brothers 'coz who else can I blame it on when I break a window? A brother is someone who disappears when it's his turn to do the dishes. The best thing about having a little brother is that you can play all the kids' games without looking too stupid. A little brother is someone who makes magic potions with your best talc and bubble bath.

RACHEL PIRTHEESINGH, AGE 12

Happiness is your brand new record by your favourite group. Unhappiness is when your baby brother sits on it.

SUZANNE STRINGER, AGE 13

BROTHERS!

Brothers *mean* to give things back.

. . .

Brothers stand on your bed to reach a
shelf – in muddy boots.

. . .

Brothers know exactly how to make you
squeal like a pig in the middle of a silent
solemnity.
And how to look absolutely astonished...
and appalled.

. . .

If anything you need is missing – check
your brother's room first.
Saves a lot of time.

. . .

The brother who drives the family insane
is the brother all the old ladies adore.

. . .

A day when a brother falls for a plastic
biscuit, a rubber fried egg or a puddle of
imitation ink on their homework is a day
never wasted.

PAM BROWN, b.1928

You can always tell which is the brother
– he's the fellow who, when everyone else is
shouting "Bravo!", "Brilliant!", "Incredible!",
"Hurrah!",
wanders up to the Star and says
"Not bad, Spotty".

PAM BROWN, b.1928

Through their clubby confidences and shared secrets, through the time they spend alone and the knowledge they gain, siblings learn to cooperate and get along together. They discover the meaning of loyalty, and master skills in defending one another against the outside even in the midst of their own angers or vicious battles. They cultivate their ability to have fun, to laugh and make jokes. They gain their first experiences in knowing themselves as individuals but also as persons connected to others. In short, they learn what it means to be "we" and not just "I".

FRANCINE KLAGSBRUN

I think, am sure,
a brother's love exceeds
All the world's loves

in its unworldliness.

ROBERT BROWNING (1812-1889)

Brothers and sisters are as close as hands
and feet.

VIETNAMESE SAYING

What can a sister safely borrow from her
brother? His toolkit? No way! Something of
his strength, though – something of his
bravery, and sense of fun. These are hers
for the taking.

CHRISTINE HARRIS

My brother, Deon. A sure pivot to my life
– how glad I am I have him.

HELEN THOMSON, b.1943

*Somewhere between Shanghai and Manila,
the sea-faring junk Joss was caught
in a cyclone and all aboard were seized with terror.
When the storm was at its height, a
god appeared and in a fearsome voice demanded
who among them were brothers.
Laughing with relief, the passengers pointed at two
who stood side by side. The god spoke
again. "Deny your brother and you may stay
aboard. Claim your bond and jump into the sea!"
Without waiting a beat of the heart,
the brothers, as if they were one, plunged into the*

turbulent waters. Deeper and deeper they sank
until their feet touched the ocean floor. But as they
bowed to bid farewell, two giant turtles
stopped before them. In no time, they rode to the
surface of the sea. One swam toward
the continent, the other toward the islands. The
great ship was gone. Nowhere to be seen
were those who had denied their bonds. The waters
were without a ripple and the skies a
luminous blue.

CLAN STORY, FROM "SPRING MOON",
BY BETTE BAO LORD

The birth of my brother, seven years my junior, instilled in me a profound sense of possessiveness, but most of all of love. As I held him in my arms I thought, "I will protect him and love him always."

LISA SCULLY-O'GRADY

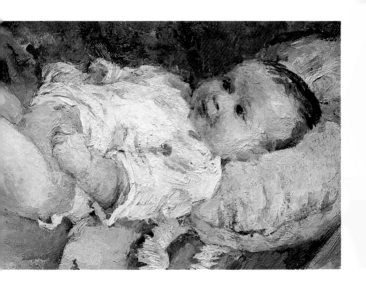

The silliest stories, the wildest adventures, the greatest kindnesses – belong to brothers.

MARION C. GARRETTY, b.1917

I copied him, I loved him, I wanted to be him.

LEO TOLSTOY, ABOUT HIS BROTHER SERGEI

Of all the needs (there are none imaginary) a lonely child has, the one that must be satisfied, if there is going to be hope and a hope of wholeness, is the unshaking need for an unshakable god. My pretty black brother was my Kingdom Come.

MAYA ANGELOU, b.1928

I sat in the window seat in the hall and waited. Unconsciously aware that I might be needed or sent for. I rifled through the glossy pages of "Boys Own" and kept one ear cocked for the awaited cry of the Baby. It was Nurse Hennessy, at the top of the stairs, who called me. Not the Baby. She was smiling and carried a white bundle. "Come up and meet your little brother!" she cried as if we were all at a party. It looked, from my point of view, like rabbit-

offal wrapped in a shawl. I was silent with shock at the sight of this living stranger in our midst. This was the bulge in my mother's belly. This the cause of the vastly disturbed household. The nursery smelled of powder and methylated spirit. She unwrapped the offal and laid it in my reluctant arms. "Hold its neck. Otherwise its head will fall off, and we don't want that, do we!" I was not altogether sure.

DIRK BOGARDE, b.1921, FROM
"A POSTILLION STRUCK BY LIGHTNING"

Mum is a good Mum. She smacks
my brother and sends him to bed.

EMMA PEARSALL, AGE 7

I like to jump on my brother and
that makes me happy.

LYNSEY SMITH, AGE 5

Most of the time my brother
collects dust watching T.V.

CHRISTOPHER BRADSHAW, AGE 9

*I'M THE YOUNGEST in our house so it
goes like this:
My brother comes in and says: "Tell him to clear
the fluff out from under his bed." Mum says,
"Clear the fluff out from under your bed." Father
says, "You heard what your mother said." "What?"
I say. "The fluff," he says. "Clear the fluff out from
under your bed." So I say, "There's fluff under his
bed, too, you know." So father says, "But we're
talking about the fluff under your bed." "You will
clear it up won't you?" Mum says. So now my
brother – all puffed up – says, "Clear the fluff out
from under your bed, clear the fluff out from under
your bed." Now I'm angry. I am angry. So I say –
what shall I say? I say, "Shuttup Stinks
YOU CAN'T RULE MY LIFE."*

MICHAEL ROSEN,
FROM *"WOULDN'T YOU LIKE TO KNOW"*

When our elders said unkind things about my features (my family was handsome to a point of pain for me), Bailey would wink at me from across the room, and I knew that it was a matter of time before he would take revenge. He would allow the old ladies to finish wondering how on earth I came about, then he would ask, in a voice like cooling bacon grease, "Oh Mizeriz Coleman, how is your son? I saw him the other day, and he looked sick enough to die." Aghast, the ladies would ask, "Die? From what? He ain't sick." And in a voice oilier than the one before, he'd answer with a straight face, "From the Uglies." I would hold my laugh, bite my tongue, grit my teeth and very seriously erase even the touch of a smile from my face. Later, behind the house by the black-walnut tree, we'd laugh and laugh and howl.

MAYA ANGELOU, b.1928, FROM *"I KNOW WHY THE CAGED BIRD SINGS"*

... young siblings become allies. They may fight and scream at each other, but they also offer one another solace and safety in a world that appears overwhelmingly stacked in favor of adults. They share secrets parents never hear, and communicate with each other through signals and codes, private languages whose meanings only they know.

FRANCINE KLAGSBRUN,
FROM "MIXED FEELINGS"

A brother somehow makes one feel secure. Anchored into life. Certain that whatever happens someone will be there to help you up, dust you down and set you on your way. A contemporary who understands your hopes and your fears. Always.

PAM BROWN, b.1928

In times of sadness, everyone searches for the right words. Except brothers. They are just there – and that's enough.

PETER GRAY

Can the single cup of wine
We drank this morning
have made my heart so glad?
This is a joy that comes only from within,
Which those who witness will
never understand.
I have but two brothers
And bitterly grieved that both were far away;
This spring, back through the Gorges of Pa,

I have come to them safely, ten
thousand leagues...
Hsing-chien, drink your cup of wine,
Then set it down and listen to what I say.
Do not sigh that your home is far away;
Do not mind if your salary is small.
Only pray that as long as life lasts
You and I may never be forced to part.

PO CHU-I (772-846),
FROM *"TO HIS BROTHER HSING-CHIEN"*

We were very close, very close and still are to this day. We were a sort of secret society, really. Being a twin gives you a unique sort of confidence; you know that wherever you are you'll be the first concern of another human being.

TONY HAMILTON, *"DAILY MAIL"*, APRIL 2, 1996

We would fight each other until an outside force intruded; then we stuck together. Sometimes my allegiance to him would go too far. If some bigger boy on the block started a fight with Warren, I would rush in like Rocky Graziano and finish him off.

SHIRLEY MACLAINE,
FROM *"DON'T FALL OFF THE MOUNTAIN"*

When brothers agree, no fortress is so strong as their common life.

ANTISTHENES (C.455-C.360 B.C.)

Your brother moans about you – but heaven help anyone else who does!

PAM BROWN, b.1928

... but this contentment was shattered when Jack was sent off to boarding school in Switzerland... Mama thought Switzerland must be "good for ears", so poor little Jack, aged seven, was taken to the station. He looked so frightened and babyish that Mama burst into tears as the train left. Momentary emotion. I knew in my bones the misery of that small figure plucked out of the nest, and I wept through night after night thinking of him.

ANITA LESLIE, FROM "THE GILT AND THE GINGERBREAD"

But you know, don't you, that I consider you to have saved my life. I shall never forget that; I am not only your brother, your friend, but at the same time, I have infinite obligations of gratitude to you for the fact that you lent me a helping hand at the time, and have continued to help me. Money can be repaid, not kindness such as yours.

VINCENT VAN GOGH (1853-1890),
TO HIS BROTHER THEO

One time when business was bad for me I was mulling things over with Geoff and he said "How much do you need?" I said £100,000. And he said: "Right, it's yours." In fact, things took an upswing but I know if I had taken it he'd never have mentioned it again. He'd never have said: "You owe me one." Never.

TONY HAMILTON, *"DAILY MAIL"*, APRIL 2, 1996

"We are able to pour out our hearts to each other" [Roy] said. "I don't think many brothers have that, and it's too bad, because many of them really care very deeply about each other." ... without trying to romanticize brotherly ties, I do want to emphasize that they often include a great deal of intimacy, affection, and empathy, and far more than is openly acknowledged and recognized.

FRANCINE KLAGSBRUN,
FROM *"MIXED FEELINGS"*

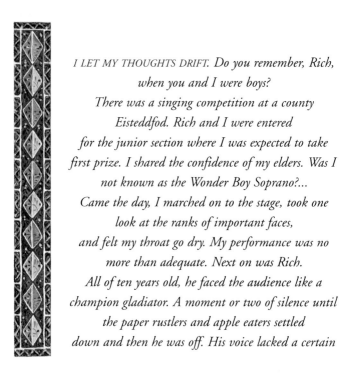

I LET MY THOUGHTS DRIFT. Do you remember, Rich, when you and I were boys?

There was a singing competition at a county Eisteddfod. Rich and I were entered for the junior section where I was expected to take first prize. I shared the confidence of my elders. Was I not known as the Wonder Boy Soprano?...

Came the day, I marched on to the stage, took one look at the ranks of important faces, and felt my throat go dry. My performance was no more than adequate. Next on was Rich.

All of ten years old, he faced the audience like a champion gladiator. A moment or two of silence until the paper rustlers and apple eaters settled down and then he was off. His voice lacked a certain finesse, but he sang and acted with pure rapture. The applause followed him all the way to the winner's rostrum, leaving me to collect the prize for runner-up. It was Rich all over. Talented, yes, but he had something more – the knowledge that winning has most to do with wanting. And he wanted to succeed very much indeed. There was another side to his character revealed that day. When the audience had dispersed and we were getting ready to go home, he came up to me, put his hand in mine and left me holding – the winner's medal. "You take it," he said, "I thought you were the best."

GRAHAM JENKINS,
FROM *"RICHARD BURTON: MY BROTHER"*

This world is too wide and lonely to be
endured without our brothers.

PAM BROWN, b.1928

How do people manage without a brother?
Someone to tell their secrets.
Someone to share their adventures.
Someone to show their acquisitions.
Someone to stick up for them.
Someone to take care of.
Someone who will be there in times of fear
or sickness and in times of joy.

PAM BROWN, b.1928

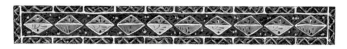

I was nearly eighteen when I left home. My brother Shiva was five and a half. Up to that time I had seen him, been aware of him, every day. For the next six years I never saw him, never heard his voice....

At home on the afternoon of my arrival, in a quiet time after the family welcome, Shiva came to me upstairs. He had after all been waiting for me to come back home. And he had something to show me; a piece of writing he had done, a story. Easily, as if it was the

most natural thing, he lay down beside me, and we read his story together. This moment with Shiva, then eleven, this welcome and affection from someone who was like a new person to me, remains one of the sweetest and purest moments of my life.

V.S. NAIPAUL, FROM *"VIEWS FROM ABROAD"*

So highly regarded... are sibling ties by both individuals and society that since earliest times they have been idealized, turned into a metaphor for the very best of human relations. We speak of the "brotherhood of man" as a paradigm of love and loyalty, of an era in which people and nations will live together in equality and justice.

FRANCINE KLAGSBRUN,
FROM *"MIXED FEELINGS"*

So incredible was our final separation that it made life itself seem unreal. I had never believed that I could actually go on living without that lovely companionship which had been at my service since childhood, that perfect relation which had involved no jealousy and no agitation, but only the profoundest confidence, the most devoted understanding, on either side. Yet here I was, in a world emptied of that unfailing consolation, most persistently, most unwillingly alive.

VERA BRITTAIN (1893-1970),
FROM *"TESTAMENT OF YOUTH"*

The feeling of solitude that overcame me in the middle of the morning on the day my brother died – some hours before I heard he had died – that feeling will probably never leave me now. It is like something at the tips of my fingers; something of which I am reminded by the very act of composition, the family vocation we shared.

V.S. NAIPAUL,
FROM *"VIEWS FROM ABROAD"*

I always needed your approval and still do.
I hope you needed me and always will.

MARION C. GARRETTY, b.1917

He's the guy I can turn to in an emergency....
We've always been able to confide in each
other, we're always in touch.

PAUL DANIELS

A kind brother can see you through a
lifetime.

PAM BROWN, b.1928

Beginning in the primeval days of childhood, even before language develops, the ties between brothers and sisters often stretch far into old age, enduring longer than any other attachment we have. Parents die, friends drift away, marriages dissolve. But brothers and sisters cannot be divorced: even if they do not speak to each other for twenty years, they remain forever connected by blood and history.

FRANCINE KLAGSBRUN,
FROM *"MIXED FEELINGS"*

Acknowledgements: The publishers are grateful for permission to reproduce copyright material. Whilst every effort has been made to trace copyright holders, the publishers would be pleased to hear from any not here acknowledged. MAYA ANGELOU: Extracts from *I Know Why the Caged Bird Sings*, © 1969 by Maya Angelou, reprinted by permission of Little Brown & Co. UK and Random House, Inc. DIRK BOGARDE: Extract from *A Postillion Struck By Lightning*, reprinted by permission of Peters Fraer and Dunlop Group Ltd. EITHNE POWER: Extracts from "Interview with Geoff and Tony Hamilton", *Daily Mail* April 2, 1996. Reprinted by permission of Solo Syndication Ltd. GRAHAM JENKINS: Extract from *Richard Burton: My Brother*, reprinted by permission of Penguin Books. FRANCINE KLAGSBRUN: Extracts from *Mixed Feelings*, reprinted by permission of Bantam Books, Inc. USA. BETTE BAO LORD: "Clan Story" from *Spring Moon*, reprinted by permission of Victor Gollancz Ltd and HarperCollins *Publishers*, USA. V. S. NAIPAUL: Extracts from "My Brother's Tragic Sense" in *Views From Abroad: The Spectator Book of Travel Writing*, ed. Philip Marsden and Jeffery Klinke. Reprinted by permission of *The Spectator*. MICHAEL ROSEN: "Wouldn't You Like To Know" reproduced by permission of Scholastic Children's Books, Scholastic Ltd.